Two Funerals, Then Easter

Two Funerals, Then Easter

A collection of poems by

Rachel Joy Welcher

For all the weary who still rejoice

Table of Contents

Old Love Letters

Survival Therapy

Chase Scenes

The Preacher

I grow low, not high
and I'll be singing
"Jesus loves me"
when I die.

Old Love Letters

It is December, and nobody asked if I was ready.

– Sarah Kay, *No Matter The Wreckage*

If I find love again

I will absolutely
celebrate it,
not in the face of those
who are alone,
but in front of those
fears that have followed me
since the day
I asked, "Are you still
in-love with me?"
And he said, "I'm not
really sure anymore."

This Is Love

Before she let me out
of the family van
she confessed
exactly what she'd been praying:
that God would give her cancer.

Crazy how our confessions
overlapped, how
we'd both been asking God
for the same thing.

"Take my life
if that's what it takes"
was my prayer for weeks
before you left me.
And for months after that.

Your mother had the same idea.
That maybe death
would shake you awake;
maybe faith
would get your attention
if it wore a hospital gown.

I know
if you read this
you will shake your head
and reassure yourself
that this
is the kind of irrational thinking
you are so glad

to be free from.

You will pity
our desperate prayers.

But I will continue asking God
to lift the scales.

I will cradle this hope,
like the child we never had.

And your mother
will keep praying
"Whatever it takes,"
remembering the way
she once
cradled you.

Because, beloved,
this is love.
It's from God.
We saw it on the cross
and that's how we knew
how to love you.
God loved us first
which is why
we love Him.
His love is the only reason
we can love anyone at all
and though we can't see Him,
we store His love
inside ourselves
and maybe one day
you'll see it.   (1 John 4:7-12)

Bones

As you picked up your bags
I could hear the sound
of zippers and regret,
too distracted by
your gracious smile
to notice the clanking
of stolen bones
and the rustling of my strength
buried loosely
beneath
your sweaters.

How It Ended

We let the background song
on the DVD menu play
over and over again
as we sat in front of the television
sideways
in the dark
looking at each other
and analyzing
plot structure

until
you couldn't stand
to hear the same tune
any longer.

Dear Old Love Letters

Please stop falling out of
my favorite books.

Please stop turning my library
into a landmine.

I tried

to imagine myself with someone else
on a park bench.
I tried
to replace that day
at the beach
on the picnic table
when you held my hand
for the first time
and peace washed over me,
warm,
like the Florida sea.
I tried
to replace what used to be.
I am trying
to be without you
but it feels empty and
cold like footsteps
on an early-morning
kitchen floor. I am trying
to reimagine what love looks like
when it is quiet
still
and alone.

I am trying.

Your Escape

All I see
are the love notes you left
like bread crumbs
scattered on the floor
leading me to an open door
then back
into an empty house.

Waiting

I'm waiting for you
to give up that clumsy,
roofless project
you call a home

so we can sit beside one another
at the table
of eternal feasts.

Please
be my dinner date
and talk to me about how it tastes,
this grace,
you thought
too good
to call true.

But True

I am at a coffee shop alone today
and I keep looking up
expecting to see him
across the table.

Sometimes I am not sure
I will ever stop expecting—
ever stop feeling
like a person divided.

Just a year ago,
we stood in our kitchen
and separated our coffee mug collection
into two separate piles.
We said:
"You can have that one. I know it's your favorite."
"You bought that one, I remember. It's yours."
And even though it made sense
I still can't make sense of it.
I still can't understand why such
a great collection of thrift store treasures
had to be divided,
packed in insufficient bubble-wrap
and taken to different states
just to mingle in separate cupboards
with other, less eccentric cups.

Today, I am drinking coffee and writing.
I am looking at the mug I am holding
and feeling empty.

I am missing cracked pottery.

This is a simple poem,
I know,

but true.

Survival Therapy

March on, my soul.

– Judges 5:21

Black Ice

For two years,
there was black ice everywhere—
on my apartment steps,
on the road to work
and on the pathway
we walked
from my car
to church.

Sometimes
we'd risk our lives
by driving down the road
to get a bag of hot tacos
to take back home.
On the way,
we'd tell stories from our day,
laugh, shiver, and
pretend
we weren't freezing.

But in the morning
I'd slip on the steps
and for the hundredth time, whisper,
"Thank you, God."

Thank you
that my neck isn't broken,
that when my car hydroplaned
through that red light,
I didn't die.
I didn't kill anyone else.

I just hovered
above ground
long enough to see
what it feels like
to lose complete control
and land again.

But winter is still
the hardest season.

Survival Therapy Tip #38

Write an email
you'll never send.

Edit it,
re-word it,
polish it like a manifesto.

Get it just right, then

leave it sitting in "drafts"
so that somewhere
those words
exist.

The Tree Outside My Window

I don't understand this half-alive tree
with beauty for branches
and a rotting core.
Each naive new shock of green
curves the trunk's bark
into a deeper,
more embarrassed smile
as if to say:
I'm sorry I didn't tell you sooner.
I'm sorry you didn't know.
I'm sorry that beauty
is fleeting
and that death
is slow.

Communion

My losses find a companion
in the man devastated
on the cross
who suffered the loss
of all things
on a rescue mission
for my soul.

He is not sympathy,
He is the Man of Sorrows.

He is not a sermon,
He is a body, broken

an embodied Psalm
of lament, *my God,*
My God…why have you forsaken me?
Be not far from me.
You are my strength;
come quickly to help me.

Those who look to Him
are dusty, like his feet
on the path to the cross,
and radiant, with faces
that will never be ashamed.

Do you feel human today?
Feed on His body,
partake of his suffering,
eat his bread: it is life.

Conversations That Are Actually Poetry #1

When your youngest brother tells you,
"God has been answering
all my prayers lately."
And you laughingly respond,
"If that's the case,
I have some things
I want you to pray for me."
And he says, "I already pray for you."
And you ask: "What do you pray?"
And he says,
"Everything."
And you say, "Really?"
And he says, "Yes."
He says, "I pray everything for you."
And you don't say
anything
because suddenly
it is hard
to speak.

In Response to Jonathan Safran Foer's Piece in the 2010 June Edition of *The New Yorker* entitled, *Here We Aren't, So Quickly*

I will never write better than I used to write
because for the first time, there is nothing boiling under the lid
of my chest.
I will turn on the lights in every room I'm not in
until I feel safe going anywhere.
I won't answer your call, because I value our friendship too
much.
I will call you back when I know I'll get your voicemail.
I will tell you to call me again.
Every year I'll buy construction paper, brand new scissors, and
double-sided tape
despite the fact that I no longer teach Kindergarten.
I'll dream of taking walks
then forget to walk when the weather is perfect.
This will go down in my mind as: *Incurable Laziness*
when it should actually be filed under: *Busy Enough to Be Forgetful*
but we all know it's true title: *Too Busy to Do the Things that Keep
You Sane—Welcome to Insanity.*
I will want to build something. Make a new friend. Take a yoga
class.
But I will find something easier and do it instead.
I will enjoy washing dishes—yet be so glad when there is not a
dish left to wash.
I will ask the stranger sitting next to me on the bus if they like
the book they are reading.
I will talk to them as long as I can.
But I will barely manage the courage it takes

just to nod at an acquaintance
in the grocery store.

Contentment

It's early morning and the sheep are out.

Sometimes their owner
lets them graze in the vineyard
near my church.

On my drive
I see them
scattered out among the vines,
mowing the in-between,
what we call weeds,
as if it were a feast

and I
could stand
to be more like them.

They
don't even notice
the grapes that will one day be wine
as they fill themselves with the grass
in their path.

To them
it is a perfect meal.

Storm Garden

Most days, I drag the hose
from the side of the house
to the backyard, but
some mornings, I wake up
to find that a storm has
already watered my garden.

Oh, Brother

When I saw you barefoot
in the backyard,
stacking your dreams higher
than the tower of Babel,
I should have warned you.

Before those bricks of hope
were scattered, confusing
the language of your future,
I should have been honest.

I'll say it now,
too late.

We don't all get to be firemen.
The first hamster you love won't be the last.
The first girl you love won't be the girl you marry.
There are things scarier
than going to camp
and things funnier
than Saturday morning cartoons.

I'm not going to be the perfect example.
Neither are mom and dad.

Christmas will be good.

But it will never hold the same magic
that it did that morning
when you ran downstairs and tore open that stuffed globe,
holding all seven continents at once.

We laughed
because it wasn't time to open presents yet
but you just couldn't wait;
so excited and impulsive,
eager to live in a world
where anything was possible.

Fragile

Your news is hollow.
An echo.
An eggshell.
A thin flower vase.
It is a brittle tree
and though
you are part
of me, dearest friend,
I cannot fix this.

Loss

Yesterday, my body
suddenly went heavy
as though my blood
had turned into sand.

Then I got your text

and understood
what my body
was already grieving.

I read your loss
like an echo to God,
"Please, be peace
that surpasses
all
earthly
understanding."

Rushed the Sand

What I do remember
is how the waves startled me
when they rushed the sand out
from under my feet,

how I gasped
and gripped
with my toes
at something
already lost
out at sea.

Graceful Bats

Tonight I watched two bats
glide just above the water
of our October lake.
They looked graceful
for Halloween creatures.
I almost didn't recognize them
as they skimmed the surface
of something so still,
deep,
and muddy.

Fuller House

It's a special kind of depression
that leads one to binge-watch "Fuller House."

Last night I was up until 2 a.m.
not laughing.

Manna

Today's manna
feels hollow
inside my stomach

but I believe You
when You tell me
that it is good, that

this food will fix
my eyes upward,
toward the skies

'til You return,
oh Bread of Life.

Psalm 88

Sometimes sorrow runs through me
like a broken hourglass,
with no small waist
to temper the pulse
of heaviness;

sending flash-floods
to rush,
stir up,
then settle, like
sand
in the coldest,
darkest
part
of God's sea.

Aloneness

I was walking to my car
with five grocery bags
cutting off circulation to my arms
when I looked up, a little too late
and crashed into Aloneness.

We had to get reacquainted.

It was awkward at first.

But pretty soon, we were back at it,
not texting anyone when we saw something beautiful
but writing poetry instead,
trying out different sleeping positions
like lying in the very middle of the bed,
reading too late,
leaving the light on,
and praying out loud
more often.

We even made up
a new game
because adults can play games too
and we called it:
ten things to do
when I'm missing you

and we played it

every night
for three months
straight.

Adventures in Grieving

Some friends
have finally stopped tip-toeing around me

having invested
in soft-soled shoes.

Dimly but Surely

It's grey outside this morning
but all the robins are singing
like they know the future
and the future is parted clouds
and flowers busting through
the uneven sidewalk by my house.

At church, I hold a toddler's hand.
It's soft and he still has dimples
above each finger. And the robins
and the baby and the sermon
that was about Moses finally
leaving the palace because
his people were in slavery
are glimpses into that old, dusty
mirror that reflects, dimly but surely,
the garden to come.

Reykjavik

America only feels
like home everywhere
when I've been elsewhere
and my pocket-size shampoo
is empty.

On my connecting flight,
in the tunnel
that connects
gate to plane
a gust of cold air
hit me in the face
and I think
there will always be
cold air
in-between; that
no matter what
where
or who
I will always be
a little lonely.

When I land at O'Hare,
for twenty seconds
Chicago feels warm
and familiar
until I enter a crowd
of walking strangers,
looking for something to eat
before their next flight.

Take a Day

It is good
to take a day
to sit by the sea
and feel
what has been battered
and renewed
again and again
into softness;

how rough rocks
and glass
now slide easily
through your fingers
into little peaks
of sand.

Stress is Fattening

chicken tacos
gyros
Cadbury eggs
cheese
lots of cheese

These are the foods
I craved
when you
were trying to decide
if you still loved me.

But this morning
I am content
with this warm,
bitter-sweet
cup of coffee.

Sipping it slowly
is a gift.

I Used To Think He Had The Kindest Eyes

I am happy in spite
of what you did
not because
of what you did

so don't ever
try to take credit
for what God
built back up
from the ashes
you left.
Theft
is what I call it
though you've convinced yourself
that it was some form of mercy.

You are not the hero
in my story.

You did not "set me free."

You crushed me.

And the only gift
I can thank you for
is the contrast you will
forever provide
between faithless and Faithful,
secrecy and intimate light;
I am alive in spite

of your sin
against me.

Your Promise to Me

My grandpa is dying.

Today I tried to make sure
my mom and aunts got rest and ate
because all they can think about
is sitting beside their father's bedside.

I made sure my grandma took her insulin.

I did my best to cook one of her recipes.

Although I am a newborn pine
among the sturdiest sequoias,
when we sang hymns
my voice had to be the strong one,
holding out the note
so they could grieve.

And at the end of this day,
I can't stop thinking about
how you should be here
being the support
and other half of me
you promised to be.

Arise

Some women create skylights
in their homes, shadow maps, so
they never forget the way. But I
shrank to the size of his expectations
for me, pulled my knees up to my chest and
told God, "You can take me home now,
only, you'll have to carry me." I was that weak.
That small. And shrinking. But instead of picking me up,
God bent down, looked me in the eyes, like
the daughter I am, and said: "Arise,
beloved one." He knew I could walk because
He had formed my legs that day He knit me together
in my mother's womb, and when He saw me wallowing
in my own blood, instead of walking away in disgust
He said, "Live! Daughter." And I did.

Years later, when I sat in the dust of what had crumbled
around me, crippled by grief, Jesus walked by and,
seeing the rubble and my legs folded underneath me,
did not hesitate to say: "Arise, daughter. Take up your mat
and walk." And I did. Because of His kindness toward me.
Because He gave me the ability to stand and
dust off the wreckage.

And on days when my legs buckle and collapse
he joins me on the floor, stoops down to sit with me
in the dust of my heartache and weariness, my Friend,
well-acquainted with grief. We don't speak,
but He is near.

And I could tell you more stories about Jesus

57

and the times he sat with me, and stood with me,
but if I wrote them all out, the world itself could not
contain the books that would be written, and
I don't need a skylight and you don't need a map
to know where the light comes from.

I don't even need a roof on this house,
because I plan
on growing much, much taller.

Live, daughter. *Arise.*

Chase Scenes

This is the widest I can stretch my arms without dropping things.

– Sarah Kay, *No Matter The Wreckage*

The Failure of Rivers & Bones

Do you ever get *so tired*
of being hurt
that even your bones
are not a deep enough
metaphor?

That spring rivers are slow
compared to how fast
you would run away
from anyone
and anything
trying to draw close?

I know
that distance
makes a lousy home.

I know that.

But somedays
it's the only direction
I am headed, the only road
open enough,
deserted enough,
to give me
the space I need.

Every Secret Drop

*Their strength is their secret. They send ferocious roots beneath the ground.
They grow up and they grow down and grab the earth between their hairy
toes and bite the sky with violent teeth and never quit their anger. This is
how they keep.*

—Sandra Cisneros, *Four Skinny Trees*

The coconut is loved for its insides.
When you crack the rock brown and push aside the thick hair,
there is meat; meat that is chalky and sweet.
The taste is mild, even weak;
diluted by fiber.
Your teeth must work hard
for a few perfumed bites.
A third layer exists that is soft,
so soft that suddenly a fruit you had to chew
becomes a drop running down your hand;
like a moment you would have enjoyed
if you'd had the chance
to anticipate it.
And you will miss it
if you are not ready with
palms cupped,
mouth wide,
or glass poised—
ready to capture every secret drop.

Sore

feet from walking where doves
flutter from the ground up
to the safety of trees
and telephone poles.
Sore
eyes from watching them.
Sore
fingers from learning the guitar
because I've always wanted to.
Sore
voice,
arms,
arms,
arms.
Sometimes joy
really does come
in the morning.

I'm falling for your joy

sharpening your depth like a pencil,
playing echo-tag with your thoughts,
while simultaneously bubble-wrapping your humor
so I can mail it to myself down the road
when you're no longer in my life.

When the padding deflates
there will be remnants
of hysterical laughter
and joy without restraint

followed by air-less memories
faded stamps
and this poem.

Unrequited love is safe

r
than you
think
ing
I'm
the one.

Help My Unbelief

I look out across Loch Ness
in search of monsters.
I'm pretty sure it's a myth kept alive
to make money from tourists and
I've read enough articles to disprove
the possibility but I still scan
the water with vigilance and when
the woman in the oversized hat
blocks my view, my heart beats
with panic that I might miss her —
that her tail might slip to
the surface for a brief moment —
that a miracle might be taking place
right in front of my eyes
and still, I would miss it.

Happy Leaves

My feelings are root-deep
always
even when I want to just
blow in the wind
like a leaf.

You are all the happy leaves
full of color and air
so annoyingly unaware
of those who live beneath you
quietly soaking up
what waters your joy

looking wearily
even *longingly*
from this heavy trunk
to your delicate veins.

This Crush (Is Really Ridiculous For Someone My Age)

Sometimes I get so excited about who you are
I forget myself.

I forget my plans,
my hands,
my age,
and my self-control in smiling.

I think about you
and become *that* person;
the cell phone in a dark movie theater,
lit up like an idiot.

While everyone else
is trying to concentrate
on what's in front of them,
I am distracted, glow-in-the-dark happy
and hating
how much I love it.

After Every Poem I Send My Mother

No, I'm not in-love with him. He's good for my poetry.

No, I'm not depressed. I *was* depressed.

Yes, that lower case "i" was intentional.

That one too.

Why?

Blame E.E. Cummings
and text messaging.
Consider it the "rebellious stage"
I never went through.

Yes, I do believe that.

No, I don't feel that anymore.

Yes, I'm going to be ok.

Yes.

You're right.

Yes.

To the One Who Let Me Get Away

"Save your breath."
That's what I heard
when you said:
"I can handle
just being friends
if that's what you need."

And I did
feel breathless that night;
the kind of
pre-hyperventilation
you get
from trying
to cushion your own fall
with a blow-up mattress
from Walmart.

I sat
in the very middle
of my empty
apartment living room,
legs-crossed, inhaling the scent
of old crackers and stale tape.
And I used
every ounce of air
I couldn't share
with you
to fill that cotton-candy blue
air mattress.

You saw

that I needed
all my strength
to soften the blow
of night-fall.

You didn't make me stay.
You let me get away.
And it remains
one of the kindest things
anyone
has ever done for me.

Pajama Party

I find that I miss you
when the crowd gets thick;
when I'm in a room
full of people
where the conversation
is quick, and the music
is just loud enough.

I know we're only just
getting to know each other.
But I think, one look
across the room at you,
would calm my inner-panic
and put my nervousness
in pajamas.

I can survive this party.
I can survive future parties, too,
if I know that at
the end of each one
I get to go home
with you.

You are the friend

I prayed for
so hard
that when God finally unclenched my fists
I almost didn't notice
the way He'd massaged them back into hands
and placed them
gently
inside of yours.

Our First Full Week Together

One of our first conversations
was about falling asleep at night
post-losing-a-spouse.
The trouble of it.
The lack of a cure.

It was nice, though,
to know someone else
was up at midnight.

During our first full week together
we started three movies
and two different TV series
without finishing a single one
because
we were so excited
to be on the same couch
because
you wanted to see my expression
and I wanted to hear your laugh
at that one scene
because
you kept falling asleep
because
suddenly you could.

Conversations that are Actually Poetry #2

"I am full of insecurities.
Just wait.
There are many more
to come,"
I joked
but needed
him to know
it was true.

"I hope
to learn all of them,"
he said

because I needed to know that, too.

In Your Sleep

Some mornings
you'll wake up
to find
that I've been
writing about you
in your sleep.

Exhausting Chase Scenes

Can we skip that part
in the movie
where they say terrible things
to each other that they
can't ever take back
and fast-forward
through the stress
of watching
one of them
chase the other
through an airport
just to apologize

and sit on your couch
in contented silence
instead?

I'd like that.
I really would.

This Fight

I think
"so many things
could go wrong."

You say,
"but so many things
could go right."

And
eventually
I'll smile, sigh,
look into your eyes,
and let you win
this fight.

Second Spring

The trees around here
are still charcoal black
from the Valley Fire
of 2015.
When spring flowers
begin to bud up
around their bases
a symbolic mix
of colors co-exist,
as loss and life
share root-space.

I start to reach
for my phone
to take a picture
of the contrast
until I remember

that I have you.

Short Kisses

I like long kisses
that I can savor and understand.
Short kisses are emojis
in a goodnight text—
nice
but not enough.

Might

I think I might like
to hold your hand in the winter,
push you off
me in the summer
and laugh about how funny
being close to someone
is.

How it's like waking up
sometimes
to soft sheets
other times
to alarm clocks
and not enough sleep.

How it's long days
and resting on couches

and how those tired-couch-conversations
turn out
to be better
than get-dressed-up dates
somehow.
Isn't that funny?

I might like it
if we take turns
tucking each other in
and pretending
we're not quite grown up yet.

I think I might like
pretending I can bake
but knowing you don't care.

I might like that;
I might like *you*.

But I don't know I don't know I don't know.
Love isn't safe.

Ache

So many memories
are a broken leg
in winter

but I miss your arms
like a smoke signal

coming
from the chimney
of a warm cabin
I know exists
just over
this snowy hill.

I guess
some absences
ache differently.

Joint Library

I keep thinking about
all the books we own, how
they might look
sitting next to each other
on the same shelf
(ok, ten shelves),

how some
might get crowded out,
double-stacked
or lost behind the couch.

I think about
how our collections
have been built up
over years, how
they are now full
of histories
short stories,
theology
and poetry;

how some pages are soft
from being read
over and over again and
others are stiff
because those books
have never been opened;
they remain
something new.

Some have marks
and notes
and expired coupons
hidden inside them.

Some
probably smell
like the summer did
the year we read them.

The one thing
I know
is that if we spent our lives
together
in this joint-library
we'd never
be without something
to read.

Treehouse

Let's live in a treehouse
where we get to climb
to bed each night
and wake up
with leaves in our hair.

Let's build shelves
around our bed
for books, made from
cousin leaves and sister trees,
and let's read until
the sun goes out.

I want to wear you like a sweater

until the hems
around my wrists
are soft and worn;
until you begin
to feel
less
like a closet item
and more
like a first choice.

I want to fuss
over how you fit
and intimidate
cold weather
by wearing you
out.

I Don't Like Dating

Maybe I could
give up over-planning
over-analyzing,
worrying myself to sleep
and just
call you up
out of the blue
and ask you to meet me
at dusk, on a bike path,
along the Pacific Coast Highway
with a bible and a ring
and a change of clothes.

In the morning
we could drink coffee
somewhere Steinbeck did
and hold hands
in the morning sunshine.

Honeymoon

I want to
warm skin kiss you
in the morning
with our eyes still half shut
in drowsy, happy rest
with nothing to do
and no place to be
but in each other's arms.

The Preacher

If you have seen the snow
somewhere slowly fall
on a bicycle,
then you understand
all beauty will be lost,
and how even that loss
can be beautiful.

– Dobby Gibson, *Polar*

"Does it bother you, how much he loved her?"

Today, he tweets pictures of her headstone,
where nestled grass has grown
over three years, and he writes
about wanting death
to come untrue;
how he'd join her some days,
if he could, how
he would like to melt
into the earth.

She was his love
and love
isn't something we bury
with dirt or time.

She was his love
and now, there will always be
loss mixed with happiness.

"Does it bother you,
how much he loved her?"

You don't ask this,
but wonder it.

And all I can tell you is that
he is a history of faithfulness;

the only future I don't fear.

The Welchers

I decided to plant fresh flowers
in the large tin pot that sits on
the stairs leading up to our front door,
and I took a paintbrush to the faded,
peeling letters scrawled across the side,
which spell: *The Welchers* in bubbly
handwriting that is not mine
or his, but hers.

Before transporting the roots and
new life, I gently removed the fall leaves
that had piled up on top of the soil,
carrying out the sacred task of
making space, then carefully retraced
what she once brightened
as a new bride in a new home,

for the roots of new flowers in a
place, precious with paint,
peeling and bright.

Your Dark Day

The hardest part
about loving
a person
who has lost
another person
is to can't-comfort-them
on the days
they just
need
to grieve,
to acknowledge
the limitation of your powers,
and wait out
the night.

Apology

I'm sorry that sometimes
when I talk about pain
I forget yours —
that, yes, you've felt that, and
yes, you know that, and deeply —
simply because
mine was different
from yours and you
don't talk as much
about all you went through.

Faces

There is no word
for this

so I will
hold your face
in both my hands
quietly.

Two Funerals, Then Easter

Two funerals during Holy Week,
as if he hasn't thought of death
enough. Last Sunday
would have been
his mother's birthday
but she died at forty-three.
Spring is when his wife died
at thirty, and lent lasts
for so long in this house that
we have to tackle each other
in hallways and our living room,
like children playing, inviting life
into bodies that have seen
too much death, forcing gloom
to surrender to joy. We have turned
laughter into legitimate therapy, which is all
our survival guide would say:

"Find someone
who cracks you up.
You'll need it."

Two funerals, then Easter
when he will remind the congregation:
He is risen.

When it's sunny, we open the front door
to watch what is growing, what is green,
what is true despite true sorrow,
and we talk about Resurrection *a lot,*
like a dear long-distance friend

who we know still loves us
despite the distance.

He is risen indeed.

And the pastor who has suffered
passes around the broken bread
of his body and heart to
a Body who needs pain recognized.

He is the gift no one prays for
because that would be cruel, but really
we are so thankful
to have you.

Marriage

We walk to church
because it's still warm
for November in Iowa
and we're not sure
how long this sunshine
will last.

We pass old houses
and talk about what we like
about each one,
the colors we'd paint them,
and the ways we'd fill up the space
in each room.

Some days are about
wanting heaven now
because it's hard to breathe
through these trials
and believe
that this vapor-life
just appears for a moment
then vanishes.

Other days
are glimpses of future glory,
taking a winter walk with my husband,
talking about our dream to start a school,
what we'll have with our steak for dinner,
how he wants me to be happy
and I am.

We hold hands,
still in our Sunday clothes,
because after church
we started to walk home
and just kept walking.

First Christmas

Slept in.
Special eggs.
Small fight.
Videos and photographs
of us opening presents
sent to family far away.
Said "Merry Christmas"
into each other's eyes
and smiles
about once an hour.
Super Mario.
I was Luigi.
I kept dying.
You were Mario.
You saved the day.
Massages.
Naps.
Spaghetti and boxed wine
while binge watching *The Office*
and trying out our new foot bath.
Christmas candy.
Stayed in our bath robes
all day, saying "Merry Christmas"
into each other's eyes and smiles
once an hour,
until it was time for bed.

Sick

at the same time,
taking turns
making tea
with body aches,
chills, and lots of TV.

I'm not happy
about anything
right now except
having you here
with me.

4 a.m.

Last night I couldn't sleep.
I didn't want to wake you
with my tossing and turning so
I grabbed my pillow and phone
and tip-toed to the guest room.

At 4 a.m., I heard the door open
and felt you climb into bed beside me.
"I missed you," you said
and you were asleep
before I could say, "me too."

I lay there
tired but awake,
sleepless, but happy.

4 p.m.

On an ordinary day
filled with papers, emails, and coffee,
he grabbed my hand and led me downstairs
without explanation.
Smiling, he kept ahold of me until we were
out the door, in the car,
and heading down the street.
I didn't ask questions,
because I'm practicing spontaneity and trust.
I let him lead me down the baking aisle
at the grocery store
and watched him throw marshmallows,
chocolates, and graham crackers into the cart.

When we got home, he lit up the Weber grill
and we roasted marshmallows
in the afternoon chill
and had s'mores
for dinner.

You are the place

where the mourning
of life gets tangled up
in fresh morning mercies;
where grocery stores and
outside chores
become adventures.

What Twitter Doesn't See

Late-night pizza with friends,
talking Star Trek and theology,
the way I rolled out the dough
the morning before to the sound
of the coffee maker and flour
got all over my shirt and some
powdered Frank's head as he
sat at my feet, waiting
for a piece of something
to fall on the floor.

The way dough rises, and other
moments of our quiet lives
that aren't trending, that are
offline, ordinary magic.

Opening a fresh set of pens, the
way my husband irons his Sunday shirt
while listening to *Pearl Jam*, and the way
the neighborhood gardens in unison
when the sun finally comes out,

and all the children on my street
are friends because it's easier
to get along when you're young
and winter has melted, and I don't
need to Instagram this
for you to believe it.

Morning Pastor

In the barely-morning
I feel a weight shift
and see his sitting silhouette
on our bed.

He gets up and
walks softly to the closet.

When he gets to the
bedroom door, he
turns the knob slowly
and I love that
I am always awake to
see the care he takes
not to wake me.

I call out for a hug
before he leaves.

He turns around,
kneels beside the bed,
and kisses my cheek.
I feel the silky tie in his hands and
am suddenly worried about
unexpected loss, funeral ceremonies
and other sad reasons we dress up, but
when I ask: "Where are you going?"
He says: "To the nursing home"
and I sigh, release my grip
and tell him "I'm glad,"
before falling back asleep.

But I am still awake enough
to hear
when he shuts the door gently
behind him.

Painting with Ash

On days when I revisit the
past, painting stories for you
with the ash, you listen,
still and intent, then quietly say:
"I'm sorry"
for things you didn't do,
and I love you.

Show Don't Tell

How many sad, hard things can we talk about
before you throw my baggage overboard
with a grunt and sigh
to make this boat go faster?

These are the questions I ask.

How many times will I need you
to remind me
that you are not him
until you get annoyed enough
to fulfill my prophecy?

These questions
are not me
but I need to know:

how long until
they become
all you can see?

Show me, don't tell me
the answer.

I'll leave the door open
just a crack
in case.

Translations

Did you know that
in some languages
"I love you"
means
"I love you"
and all one
has to do
is stop looking
for divergent translations
in order to grasp
the full meaning
of the phrase?

I didn't.

But I'm learning.

First Three Months

Last night was rough,
a one-way snowball fight
between me and my insecurities.
I threw. You watched
each one crash, tumble, and
gain momentum before
you could reply or
assure me that this cold
isn't going to last forever.

I feel like my brokenness is breaking everything.

This morning, the sun
came out, and I have never
been so thankful to sit outside
without wearing a coat.

We sat together on a bench
in the church parking lot
in silence, holding hands
in the winter sunshine,
in-love and
in pain.

Thank you for loving me
not just through this
but *in* this,
however long it takes.

There is no aloneness

quite like being sad
when you're supposed to be
happy.

Find Yourself a Husband Who Prays

Can't pray but I
lay my head on his lap
and he strokes my hair,
asking God for things
I need but can't articulate,
because the news is too much.
Because my soul is too heavy.
Because I can't speak out loud
the truth of this.

My thoughts shudder and reel
as he talks softly into my hair
to God
for both of us.

Depression

You bought me the right boots
and yesterday, we took a walk
at 3 p.m. because you know
how much it helps me
to be outside, surrounded
by God's creation.

We analyzed
the tracks different animals
had left in the snow.

We walked a path
that a rabbit, dog, cat,
and – we think - a raccoon,
had already travelled.

I could see where
the rabbit hopped to
the other side of the street.

I pointed this out to you
and you noticed too, nodded
and smiled as we talked about
the things we were seeing;
the things right in front of us.

Thank you.

Tangled

When will you realize, oh my soul,
that there will always be a child
born on the same day that
someone else dies?

That it is not selfish to be happy,
even with wreckage
in your rear-view?

That it is not within your power,
to untangle joy from pain?

Him

I found someone who,
after watching forests burn,
animals run for their lives,
and cinders light up
the night just to see
clearly enough
to extinguish life,
still thinks
there is goodness
to be found
in the land of the living.

And I
plan to hold onto him
even as trees burn
like candles.

Her

What if, once you are born
you don't like to cuddle?
What will I do
with my scoop-em-up love,
and all the stories I want to
read aloud, with you in the crook
of my arm, wide-eyed and cozy
and warm, next to me?

What if you're too
independent for that
and you play for hours
alone, stopping only for juice;
asking only for help when
you can't reach something?

That would be hard
but I would be proud of you.

My arms would ache
but I would understand.

A Lullaby

I want to kiss the darkness
from your eyes,
sing them soft and blue,
dance them into laughter
and tease them into moons.
I want to whisper them
until the lids
are heavy and full of sleep;
tell you its fine to keep them closed,
as you lay it all down
at His feet.

In the dead of winter

If I'm honest, this has been
a long, cold winter
for a Californian and I
listen eagerly when
the grocer tells me about
spring in Iowa, how
everything grows, everything.

I can't wait to see that.

For now, I take vitamin D so that
I can get out of bed when
the sun never comes out, and
I watch you raise flower beds
inside our living room with your
low chuckle and constant warmth;
you make watching TV with
blankets covering our shivering feet
feel like the place I'll go the
next time some conference speaker
invites the audience to think
about their "happy place."

You can't wait to plant us
a garden, but you already
bring life into this winter
house, this February snow globe.

Even when it's not yet green
outside, your arms are the kind
of limbs children build treehouses

118

on –
that strong, that safe, that much
of a sure thing, you bring
spring
into my life
in the dead of winter.

A Poem Dedicated to Your Low Chuckle

It's the best sound
I've ever heard, your low
chuckle and crinkled eyes -
the way your laughter
lightens everything
that is heavy in life.

The way you pulled the
car over yesterday and
bought us ice cream cones
before dinner

and we walked down a
bike path covered in leaves
and I found a caterpillar
that looked as soft as
a winter blanket.

You laughed at me as
I tried to guide it with
a stick, and our joy
mingled together.

Selah.

World weary couples

go to bed at 10
and sometimes drink wine
out of coffee mugs.
When they can't sleep
they trace letters
with their fingers
on one another's backs
and talk about tomorrow
while it is still today.

To Frank

Shelter workers found you
chasing melting snow
down the side of the road.

Even when you were lost,
you knew how to be happy.

Yesterday you made a nest out of
two blankets and a rug and took
your fourth nap of the morning. Then
you woke up and ate three peach slices
that I dropped on the kitchen floor,
because you know what it means
to be happy.

Mercy, Flickering

Mercy is the shiny thing
in the window, the warm
fire on a snowy night.

It draws a shivering crowd
of shoppers. Invites the
holiday-lonely to form
a circle around it.

Sometimes, surrounded,
its flame begins to flicker
out. But instead of stoking
the fire, the people, appeased,
scatter to find another source
of warmth in sight

and I am left low and flickering.

Oh God, be my light.

Still Shaking After All These Years

I am two-thousand-words-to-say-I-love-you
and he
just
grabs my hand,
touches my cheek,
says: "I love you, baby"
as he falls asleep.

It's exactly what I need.

But still, I drive myself crazy
wondering: *What's on his mind?*

Trying to believe him
as I sweep up any
shards of confidence
I can find into my bare hands.

He is the kind of love
that never forgets
to bring flowers home
from the grocery store,
but I am shattered peace
that echoes.

Pain still ripples my lake.

And some nights
I still shake
from the suddenness of grief

as he kisses my head,
pats my hand,
and falls asleep.

Rubble

Sometimes I think about the
ease with which you picked me up
where my life left off, how you
loved me at disenchanted
and carried me past the place
where my house caved in,
unruffled by the rubble, eager
to set me down at last in a
home, already warm with life.

At One Year

Early October is when I made sure
the twinkle lights reached across
the church courtyard and that
the shoes I ordered online
matched my wedding dress.

It's when I finished packing up all
my books and explained to my cat,
Elliot, that he would be happier if he
stayed in California with my parents.

It's when the cool air cleared away
the relentless summer and reminded
me of the grace of seasons, of the God
who stays near in the in-between.

It's when I eagerly waited for my bridegroom
to arrive, put on his suit, and make and receive
the promises that bind souls together before God,
so he could take me home to make a home, together.

One year later, the chill of October arrives,
shivering leaves off their branches, reminding me
that the locusts are gone, and that the goodness
of the Lord can be seen here in the land of the living.

And I stand in the kitchen, hugging him for warmth
as our morning coffee brews, whispering quietly into
his shoulder for the thousandth time, a prayer of thanks
to God for the gift of this season, this man, this love.

Two Trees

we are two trees
that grew up
beside one another

close enough
to string a hammock

between

us
there is only

the rest
and sway
of easy cotton

the sun lying down
on the top layer
of our skin

and
relief

that lets loose
into our palms

like heavy fruit
off the newborn branch

we are weightless

when the ropes
are tied

The Preacher

Today, in the middle of church,
the power went out
across town and I watched
Evan preach in the dark
by candlelight.

One boy bounced
a helium balloon against the pew
behind me while a baby cried
and the elderly leaned forward to hear
my husband read:
"Now faith
is the assurance of things hoped for,
the conviction of things not seen."

And I know
that faith is not by sight
but some days, I need a sign

and he gives faithfulness a body.

Old and New

A lot of things look like love
until the vase that holds the flowers
is shaken and
bitter water spills out,
covering even
the good memories.

Which is why, when I found
that old letter taped inside a
book of Pablo Neruda poems,
I made the choice to
crinkle up the past, asking God
to take care of the water damage,
to hold my future,
and to steady what still shakes
from time to time.

I asked him to be a Father,
not a love poem,
to be a doctor who makes
the tough decisions
so that, one day, I will heal.

A few hours after I threw
away that letter from my ex,
my precious husband of four months
walked into my office with
an envelope containing a poem
he'd written for me on
smooth, cream colored paper.

He didn't notice the crumpled
memory in my trash can, just smiled
and said: "I wrote this for you."

It's ok to not look back.
It's ok to look forward to the future
with a broken heart and a limp.
Is there any other way to
travel toward God
this side of heaven?

Acknowledgements

Black Ice previously appeared in *RedFence Magazine.*

Faces, Second Spring, Take a Day, Our First Full Week Together, and *"Does it bother you, how much he loved her?"* previously appeared in *Fathom Magazine.*

A special thanks to those who helped edit this collection: Jonathan Minnema, Janice Thompson, Kaitin Ruiz, Aarik Danielson, Laura Kauffman, and Joshua Torrey.

Cover Art: Acrylics on canvas by Rachel Joy Welcher

Author photo by Evan Welcher

About the Author

Rachel Joy Welcher is an editor at *Fathom Magazine* and the author of "Blue Tarp" (*Finishing Line Press*, 2016). She recently received her Master of Letters in theology from The University of St. Andrews and currently lives in Glenwood, Iowa with her husband, Pastor Evan Welcher, and their dog, Frank.

Made in the USA
Lexington, KY
28 September 2019